THE
Archive Photographs
SERIES

HEMEL HEMPSTEAD

THE
Archive Photographs
SERIES

HEMEL HEMPSTEAD

Compiled by
Eve Davis

TEMPUS

First published 1995
Reprinted 2004

Tempus Publishing Limited
The Mill, Brimscombe Port,
Stroud, Gloucestershire, GL5 2QG
www.tempus-publishing.com

British Library Cataloguing in Publication Data.
A catalogue record for this book is available from the British Library.

ISBN 0 7524 0167 X

Typesetting and origination by Tempus Publishing Limited.
Printed in Great Britain.

Contents

Acknowledgements

John Ambrose, Den Bailey, K. Barton, Peter Benton FSIA, Mrs D. Brooks, Roy Chapman, R. Critchley, Vera Dormer, Jim Elborn, D. Farmborough, R. Fonge, Mr and Mrs Glover, Ron Green, J. Hollick, Mrs Hopkins, Mrs Jennings, J. Lawson, Mrs Lee, Mrs Lord, Mrs Marin, Mr and Mrs Minty, Mrs Newton, Mr and Mrs Norman, Chimp Norman, J. Picton, J.H. Purves, E. Sammes, B. Sangster, Selden Family, Mr Sells, Mrs B. Smith, Mr W. Smith, Jeff Thorne, R. Tomkins, Mrs S. Watts, F. & V. Willmore, British Paper Co., *Hemel Hempstead Gazette*, Hemel Hempstead Library, Mr Stubbington, Miss E.M. Dale, Mrs Charman, Mrs I. Sabey, M. Ousely, Mrs Harris, London Transport Museum, Atlas Copco.

I dedicate this book to my dear family and friends and my new grandson, Ben.

Introduction

Hemel Hempstead has been regarded by many as just a New Town Development but it has a long history going back to pre-Roman times.

The town lies in the valleys of the River Bulbourne and Gade on the edge of the Chilterns in some of Hertfordshire's most attractive countryside.

In the eighth century, Hamelhampteade (one of many spellings) was a small but important village and is later mentioned in *Domesday Book* as having enough meadow to support flour plough teams and four mills worth 37 shillings and fourpence (£1.87). It was a rich wheat-growing and cattle-producing area.

The building of the parish church of St. Mary began in 1140 and took about 40 years to complete. Its fluted leaded spire is one of the highest in the country at almost 200 feet to the gilded weathervane, which was not built until much later in the fourteenth century. There are several memorials in the church, including those of the Combe family who entertained Henry VIII at Bury Manor. The King granted the town its first charter in 1539, which gave Hemel Hempstead the right to hold a weekly market on Thursdays, an annual fair on Corpus Christi, and created a court of Pie Powder (dusty feet), a way of dealing with traders' disputes there and then.

Other charters followed over the years, from Queen Elizabeth I in 1572, James I in 1609, Cromwell in 1656, Charles II in 1666, William and Mary in 1693, and in 1898 the Victorian charter, which was suitably celebrated during 1948.

In 1953, remarkable Medieval wall paintings were discovered in some cottages at Piccotts End, now restored and preserved. In these cottages the first infirmary was founded by Sir Astley Paston Cooper in 1827, but it soon became too small for the district's needs. Sir John Sebright built an infirmary in Marlowes in 1831 which in turn was converted into Kings College Convalescent Home and re-named Cheere House in 1878. It became a training school and nurses' home from 1946. Another hospital building was opened by the Duchess of Teck in November 1877 to meet the growing town's population, still part of the present hospital complex. The Prince of Wales laid a foundation stone in 1926 and the Queen Mother opened a new out-patients' block in July 1959.

St Paul's Hospital opened in 1835 as a workhouse called Hempstead House, also known as 'The Base' by locals. It was the main maternity unit for a number of years. The Tudor wing at West Herts was opened in 1987 and all patients were moved from St Pauls in 1990. The old buildings have since been demolished and the site re-developed for housing.

John Dickinson had the largest number of employees working at Apsley Mills. From small beginnings in 1890 the numbers reached 5,0000–plus in the early 1950s. The Guildhouse was built in 1920 and its dining rooms were filled with workers at lunchtime, and it was the venue for many inter-departmental socials, dances, and concerts.

No-one can forget the masses of cyclists who used to flood the roads at home time. Lines of buses were always ready to take workers to all areas of the town. J.D.'s had their own efficient Fire Service, who won numerous cups and shields. The Dickinson Apsley Band was founded in 1894 and in their heyday also won awards and cups at contests at Belle Vue and the Royal Albert Hall. Between the wars they broadcast on the BBC. Shendish House and grounds are remembered with affection for many things, including many sports facilities and a place where employees could relax. There was even a small bus which went from the main road up to the house and back – no cars in those days.

A large part of Dickinsons moved to newer premises on the other side of the canal in Belswains Lane; the old buildings were demolished and cleared, being replaced with a large Sainsbury's and other warehouse-type businesses.

In 1947, the new town industrial area grew fast when factories of all kinds moved from London to Hemel and gave workers a vast range and choice of jobs and a modern house. Neighbourhood communities grew at Adeyfield, Bennetts End, Chaulden, Highfield, Gadebridge, and Warners End. Grove Hill and Woodhall were built later.

Marlowes has again been largely rebuilt with a covered shopping mall scheme and pedestrianisation, several new features have been added: statues, modern sculpture, a children's play area, and an information centre. There is a fountain near bank court and many seats dotted about which encourage people to sit and chat, and in the summer months entertainers perform. The trend of out-of-town supermarkets has altered some people's shopping habits, causing several small shops to close or move into a unit within the mall. The market place has had a face lift and ornamental paving has added interest.

Hemel Hempstead is well-known for its 'funny roundabout', and during the construction the course of the river was altered to run through the middle of the central island when enlarged to accommodate six mini roundabouts. The new system came into force in June 1973 and works very well. Its future was threatened recently but several petitions and protests forced the planners to think again.

The town is now surrounded by a motorway network. The M1 and M25 are the major motorways connecting London to the rest of the country and the airports of Heathrow, Gatwick, Luton, and Stansted. The new A41 has proved worthwhile and relieved through traffic in Kings Langley and Berkhamsted. With Hemel Hempstead only being 25 miles from London, it takes an average time of thirty minutes for the rail commuter to reach London Euston.

Interest in nostalgia is still popular and the changes to Hemel Hempstead need to be recorded to help people remember what was in place before recent new developments – after all, it is history in the making.

One
Marlowes and High Street

The Plough, *c.* 1880. The junction of Two Waters Road and Station Road. The Heath Park railway bridge is just visible beyond the trees on the right of the photograph. The house was the home of the Carey sisters, founder members of the Baptist Church at Two Waters. This area is also known as Moor End.

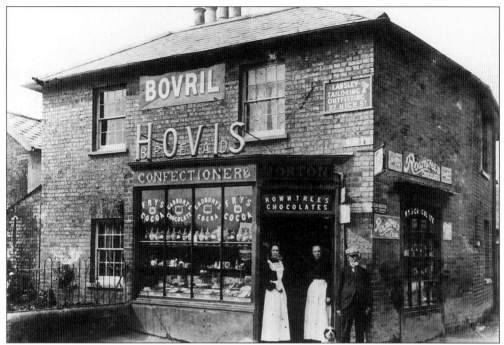

This corner shop at Moor End was owned by Mrs Elizabeth Morton, *c.* 1912. She is possibly one of the ladies at the door. It was later run by the Sells sisters, Lizzie and Annie. Underground springs abound in this area and it was frequently flooded after heavy rain, but this did not stop customers buying their sweets and ice cream.

The Plough pub, which gives this area its name, *c.* 1950s. Looking towards Marlowes and the railway viaduct, through which can be seen the construction of the Co-op. A road widening scheme at this time saw the demolition of the cottages and small shops.

A later view of the railway viaduct spanning Marlowes, which was a splendid landmark to the entrance to the town. The Hemel Hempstead & Harpenden branch line ran until complete closure took place in 1959. Large crowds gathered on 6 July 1960 when the bridge was blown up at midnight. Alderman A.H. Jarman lived in one of the houses on the extreme right.

Lower Marlowes, 1950s. Looking towards the bridge from the opposite direction. Moore's shoe shop; Hemmings, tobacconists; Moorecroft, greengrocer; Fortnum, butcher; Garments, grocer; Smiths, picture-framer; and Harris, barber, were the shops that lined the road. This is approximately where Marks & Spencer now stands.

Marlowes, 1933. A.W. Rowden, outfitters and drapers, was completely gutted by fire. It was a popular shop in the town and at sale times bargains and novelties could be had for 3d and 6d. The fireman is Mr Williams. The shop was reconstructed and later became Hendersons. Next door was Frank Chapman, chemists, and Miss Edmunds, shoe shop.

Luxor Cinema, 1960. First opened in 1926, it was called New Aero. It changed its name to Luxor when new sound and screen were installed. The Operatic Society used it for some of their productions. W.W. Saunders garage moved to Moor End and later became Shaw and Kilburn. Woolworths is in the process of being built and is still there today. Sainsbury's and Timothy Whites were the shops that came later.

The Post Office.
Hemel Hempstead.

129954

Marlowes, 1937. This new Post Office opened in May 1937 to replace the smaller and outgrown premises in Alexandra Road. The Salvation Army Citadel was next door, and moved to new buildings by the market in Waterhouse Street. On the left side of Marlowes were large private houses which also gave way to development for shops.

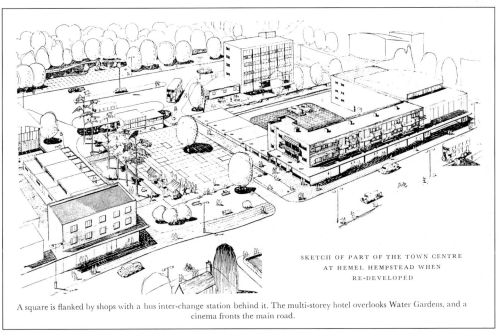

SKETCH OF PART OF THE TOWN CENTRE
AT HEMEL HEMPSTEAD WHEN
RE-DEVELOPED

A square is flanked by shops with a bus inter-change station behind it. The multi-storey hotel overlooks Water Gardens, and a cinema fronts the main road.

This sketch gives an interesting idea of what the planners had in mind for the New Town in 1952. This was to be the market square with shops surrounding it and a multi-storey hotel near the bus station. In reality the hotel became the King Harry pub.

The White House, *c.* 1900. A survey map of 1898 shows the building in existence then in Marlowes. It is remembered as Hartridge & Roe, furniture store, later just as Hartridges. The narrow turning on the right was Fernville Lane (or Nannygoat Lane), today known as Midland Road. The building is now offices and a photocopying service.

This large house was off Fernville Lane, tucked round the back of houses in Marlowes. Fernville House was a private residence and later divided into flats. The house and grounds were cleared for re-development. The lawns were carefully lifted and the turfs used for the 'Funny Roundabout'. The site is now the Somerfield supermarket.

14

No. 78 Marlowes, *c.* 1920. These were the premises of A.L. Selden, an established family firm of builders founded in 1908. The business passed to his son Charles in 1936 when he retired, and is now in the hands of the third generation of the family. Councillor Selden was Mayor and Bailiff of Hemel Hempstead, 1945–48.

This group of shops at the end of Marlowes was built in the late 1930s and is known as Central Parade. Many of the shops have changed since then and are mostly estate agents, although the Midland Bank is still there. The buildings on the opposite side of the road – except for the Methodist church – were demolished to make way for Dacorum College.

Six Bells, Bury Road. From 1906 to 1927, Henry Turner was the landlord. His son-in-law James (Jim) Sangster took over until 1954, when it was pulled down for new roads and development. On the left was Sid Williams' sweet shop, tobacconist, and newsagent and barbers run by Sid Pollard. Elliotts were the original brewers in the mid-1860s.

Old Police Station, Bury Road, *c.* 1860, soon after the Police were installed here from Queen Street. The building looks very smart with plants and shrubs around the main entrance. In the 1920s there was one superintendent, two sergeants, and twelve constables. When the new police station was built in Combe Street in 1958, the old building became probation offices.

Looking up the High Street at the junction of Queen Street (Queensway) and the Broadway, *c.* 1890. At one time there were 24 pubs and beer houses in the street. Only a few remain today: the White Hart, Rose & Crown, the Bell, and the Kings Arms. Lloyds Bank, an imposing building, was built in 1882.

High Street's Coronation or Silver Jubilee Decorations, c. 1930's. Boro' Ironmongers moved to premises in Marlowes in 1937.

A rear view of Kings Arms, High Street, c. 1950, a seventeenth-century listed building. Straw plait was sold in the yard in the 1830s and entertainers would perform from the balcony.

6056. BRACKETT'S SHOP, 23, HIGH STREET.

High Street, *c.* 1890. Looking south towards Queen Street (now Queensway). Joshua Brackett's Stationers and Printers had been established since the 1870s and continued until well into the 1920s. He was also a bookbinder, and sold sheet music.

Henry Hancock, Plumber, *c.* 1880. This business was listed in *Kelly's Directory* as early as 1869 and continued until the late 1920s. This shop down the dip in the High Street later became the Flower Box and was made famous on television as a location for a series called *Pie in the Sky*, when the frontage was changed to that of a smart restaurant.

Two

Around the Town

Leverstock Green in the 1945–50 era. The Leather Bottle, on the right, is only half its present size. The houses between to the White Horse have gone to make way for the village shopping parade and petrol station. Today, the grass is kept shorter and there is now a pavement on the left side of Bedmond Road.

Cox Pond, Adeyfield, c. 1955. Cox Pond Farm and land was compulsorily purchased in 1948. During the war the farm land was worked by Italian POW's. The pond was very large and deep and had been used for testing the waterproof quality of vehicles used in the D-Day landings.

Adeyfield, 1949. The first-developed neighbourhood was Adeyfield with the Industrial Estate beyond. Houses were built in a variety of styles and sizes to aim at a balanced community. Where possible, existing trees were left to set off the buildings and to improve the landscape.

Development in the industrial area began in 1949. Many firms moved from London into purpose-built factories. Atlas Copco's first building in the early 1960s almost looks like a model – note the lack of vehicles and road markings in Maylands Avenue.

Corner Farm, High Street Green, *c.* 1955. Had been a farmhouse for 400 years and was reverted to a private house in 1979. A bakery business was there for a while and in the 1980s it was proposed that the building should be converted into a restaurant, craft museum and real ale brewery.

Piccotts End, 1926. The hamlet where a small hospital was founded by Sir Astley Paston-Cooper in 1827. This soon became too small and a new building was erected in the town and became part of West Herts Hospital. In 1953 Medieval wall paintings were discovered in cottages here, now restored and preserved.

Old cottages at Water End in the early part of this century. Heavy through-traffic is the main problem for the residents of this hamlet today.

The premises of Barrett Gardiner, local photographer in Alexandra Road, before modernisation in the 1930s. Later pictures show large windows and a central door. The business continued until 1952, when Mr Gardiner retired.

Alexandra Road, *c.* 1928. The gabled building was the town's main Post Office for over thirty years before it moved to Marlowes in May 1937. Lower down are small shops, including the *Gazette* newspaper offices. St Mary's spire can just be seen over the rooftops.

Alexandra Road shops, c. 1950. Ball's furniture shop; Foxall, grocer; Fullers, boot and shoe repairs; Pyle and Thompson, radio and TV. Leading to the Doctor's surgery, a group practice including Dr Gilruth and Dr Gregory.

Midland Station, 1901. An enthusiastic welcome being given to Hemel Hempstead Volunteers having returned from the Boer War, arriving at Midland Station.

London Road, *c.* 1912. The draper's shop was run by Mr John Mann and his wife, Mary. Next door was the Oxford Club Brotherhood, a thriving Bible Class group for men. Miss Marnham was the secretary for a number of years.

London Road, *c.* 1906. Boxmoor Baptist Church was built in 1864 to replace an earlier and smaller chapel. This area was called Duckhall. John Sygrave, baker and beer retailer, and Thomas Howard, grocer, were next door to a dairy which later became the Hygienic Dairies. Further along was William Glover, coal merchant. The boys in the photograph seem about to play ball games.

Two Waters Bus Garage, 1935. There was no garage at Hemel Hempstead at all until 1933 when a shed was rented in Bury Road. 1935 saw the building of a new garage at Two Waters to hold 50 buses. An outline plan in 1949 proposed the bus station would have a new railway passenger station built alongside, which would replace the present Apsley & Boxmoor stations.

Old Boxmoor Station, c. 1960, pictured just before demolition in the mid-1960's to make way for a modern station.

Lockers, 1906. This old building has a long history. It was a hunting lodge around 1550 and was converted to a gentleman's residence by Ebenezer John Collett, who purchased it in 1799. In the late 1920s it became a school for young ladies with Miss Simmonds as principal. It was used by Cavendish School as a sixth form annexe. The building has been sold to developers, who may change it into flats.

Hammerfield, around 1900. It had many names including Little Switzerland owing to the many fir trees that had been planted on the land in the previous century. Some of the houses that were built here were left incomplete and remained so for many years. St. Francis' Church was not built until 1908, and a larger one was opened in 1914. The older building is now the church hall.

Bridge Street, *c.* 1948. J.F. Stone, Coal and Corn Merchants, began trading just after the First World War, and later became a general stores. Bridge Street was one of the first roads to be demolished for New Town Development.

Cotterells, *c.* 1905. Taken from the junction of Cemetery Hill leading to Bridge Street on the right. The long row of houses remains today with improved outside maintenance. The yard and buildings were used by the council as a parking lot. All has now been demolished and cleared, opening up the view across the Leighton Buzzard Road to the town centre.

Corner House at the bottom of Cemetery Hill and Cotterells, *c.* 1910. The older lady was Mrs Ada Baldwin, who ran a laundry in brick out-buildings (now demolished). The man on crutches was Tom, one of her sons, who was a boot and shoe maker working from the same premises. The young woman by the gate is Bessie Baldwin, possibly her youngest daughter. It is not known who the young ladies on bicycles are, but assume they are more daughters. They were a large family with several sons serving in the Army in India.

Three
Apsley

Apsley between 1895 and 1900. Looking across the Salmon Meadow towards a very rural village, long before it was developed into an industrial area. The Church of St. Mary, Apsley End, dominates the skyline.

London Road, Apsley, c. 1927. The parade of shops on the left is still there, although changes of trades have taken place. Some of the names remembered are Buckle, greengrocer; Tommy Court, furniture and hardware; Druce, butcher; Stratford, boots and shoes; and W. Runham, draper and haberdashery. The White Lion must be one of the original pubs still trading today.

Rickmaking in 1887 on the site of what is now Apsley Station.

34

The very beginning of Apsley railway station being constructed for the benefit of workers of John Dickinson's in 1938. It was opened on 28 September of that year by a special train that broke through a screen of Croxley paper stretched across the rails. This event made the front cover of the *Dickinson News*.

Going home from Apsley Mills along the London Road, *c*. 1904. The large house in the foreground belonged to Kents brushmakers and further along stands the Fountain pub.

The British Paper Co., Frogmore Mills, about 1924 soon after the new office was built. The firm was founded in 1890 and celebrated its Centenary in 1990. The houses and gardens in the foreground have all been swept away and it is now a large place for car parking.

The British Paper Company Fire Brigade, *c*. 1913, with their Shand Mason steam-powered fire engine. Mr Cecil Sanguinetti is in the front row with his hand on his belt.

Another view of Salmon Meadow, Apsley, between 1914 and 1920. John Dickinson's paper mills buildings are beyond the Apsley Football Club's original ground, which later went to Crabtree Lane and in time became Hemel Hempstead Football Club.

This new Card and Board Department at Apsley was begun in 1933 and covered all that was left of the old 'Salmon Meadow'. This too has now all gone and is part of Sainsbury's supermarket.

Card Dept. staff outing, 1949. Some in the group are Ted Neal, George Plummer, Greta ?, Mr Delderfield, Mr Bonfield, Jim Grace, Les Burnham, Mr Sygrave, Amy Parrish, Tony Charge, Rosemary Parrish, Connie Cook, Grace Thorpe, Eve Nice, Phillip Wyatt, Daphne Mole, Miss Liddiard, Kath Mudd, June Arnott, Kath Potton, Arthur Grimsdale, Josie ?, Alan Crawley.

London Road Apsley *c.* 1914. No traffic problems here. St. Mary's Church and on the left the Parish Rooms where meetings, socials and wedding receptions were held.

London Road, Apsley, *c.* 1912, opposite Kent's Brush Factory and the Fountain pub. John Worth's Grocer and Refreshment Rooms show brand names still with us. An early filling station is next door. These premises are now a display and signwriter's shop. Three small cottages were tucked behind these buildings and at this time the families living there were Sells, Cook, and Dolt.

John Dickinson & Co., *c. 1960*. The large white building is the envelope department. The brick building in the foreground was the firm's canteen before the Guildhouse was built in 1920. It later became a Day Continuation School, in May 1946, until the need diminished when Dacorum College was opened. The building then became Wages Dept.

The building of Book Department at Apsley Mills. The new factory and office was in construction by 1927 and completed in 1930 at a cost of £12,000. The canal was very important for the delivery of coal and timber to the mills.

Apsley Mills, *c.* 1963, showing the railway and Apsley Station, the old A41 and John Dickinson & Co. from Doolittle to Card Dept. Most of this has all been swept away for re-development and apart from some buildings surrounding the cottage, it has all transferred to the new Stationary Dept on the other side of the canal in Belswains Lane.

Nash Mills House, *c.* 1790, which was lived in by the Dickinson family until 1834, followed by Mr & Mrs Longman, who later moved to Shendish. John Evans, another member of the family, also lived there. The house was turned into offices in 1906.

Cottages at Doolittle Apsley were built in 1826. The nearest cottage in this row of six was lived in by Mary Fortnum (née Sangster). There were twelve houses in all, with a pump in the centre. They were demolished in the 1930s and the site became a car park for John Dickinson and is now a business park of the same name.

Four
Boxmoor

The corner of Cowper Road and St John's Road, *c.* 1900. Marshall's chemist shop. Well known for his own patent medicines, he also kept bees and was often called out to collect a swarm. The lady at the gate is Mrs Marshall, who ran a kindergarten in a room at the back of the house.

Newly completed houses in Cowper Road, *c.* 1914, in the days when road surfaces were rough and a horse and cart was the only traffic. Lee & Smith, Builders & Decorators' signboard can just be seen on the left. The houses lost their railings in the Second World War, when they were removed to help the war effort.

The same corner in the early 1960s. The house and chemist shop (Shields & Warren) being demolished to make way for a garage and petrol station. The greengrocer closed in 1994 and the Bank closed in 1993 having been there since 1937. It is now an estate agent's.

St. John's Road looking west, 1908, before the road was widened and houses lost some of their front gardens. The flint cottages on either side of the road are still intact and apart from the Chemist corner, no major changes have been made and it is recognisable today.

St John's Road. H.P. Porter High Class Grocers, c. 1930s. Bacon and ham was sliced to order and biscuits were sold from glass-topped tins. Jim Gray, the manager, is standing outside the shop. It changed to a small self-service until 1980 and opened as a locksmiths in 1981.

In 1897, James Loosley came to 87 St John's Road. This is possibly his son standing in the doorway. W. Charman took over in 1926 and his son Jim carried on until his own retirement. It traded as a butcher until closure in 1994. The premises are now a hairdressers.

St. John's Road in the 1950s. Houses and shops are virtually unchanged except for some modern windows. The draper's shop is still sorely missed for all the haberdashery and wool sold there. Mrs Richie was the last owner before it changed to an off-licence. Up to 1906, post office business was conducted there, until the new premises were built in Horsecroft Road.

St John's Road. Ranscombe's was one of a cluster of buildings on the corner of Anchor Lane. The family ran the bakery business from around 1906 up to the 1940s. When Mrs Ranscombe died, the shop closed and was later demolished when a road-widening scheme took place in the 1950s.

Catholic Church of St Mary & St Joseph in the 1960s. This church was first opened in 1898. The barn of Proctor's Dairy can be seen, and there is no footpath on the right-hand side of the road. One of the oldest pubs, the Three Blackbirds, has been modernised and a raised footpath runs alongside the property.

Fishery Lock, *c.* 1906. Fishery Stores ran by the Austin Brothers did a brisk trade with the boat people on their way to and from London and Birmingham on the Grand Junction Canal. The bridge shown here replaced a wooden one in 1876.

This attractive balustrade bridge was completed in 1927. The Fishery Inn and shop continued with passing trade from the canal and also commercial travellers used the inn when travelling by train and needing an overnight stop. Widening of this bridge and road began in January 1969, which also meant that this bridge had to go and be replaced by a modern one.

Fishery Road, Boxmoor before the road changes in the 1960s. The Fishery Inn has had several alterations and was once an important place for stabling horses. In adjoining buildings, Anderson & Woodman had a corn chandlers' business and nearby there was Keen the coal merchant. On the extreme left were Hollicks watercress beds, which later became Draper's The low building in the centre was known as Kelly's forge, then Hay's engineering and now a glass and mirror shop.

Fishery Cottages near the Forge were often flooded because of the many underground springs. They were demolished in 1969 and the cleared site left for several years. A block of modern houses now occupy this area. The footpath at the side of the houses lead to the Guide Hut and on up to Butcher's Alley and Boxmoor Village. It is a short cut used by local commuters for the railway station.

A view of the canal, Boxmoor, *c.* 1925. This part of the canal shows saplings of willow being grown for use in the making of cricket bats. Some of the Moor or Star cottages are in the background and were demolished in 1933. A few of the houses in St John's Road are just visible. Chestnut trees have been planted in avenues for some of the Coronations and grown into mature trees throughout the moor.

These cottages stood in front of Boxmoor Station and were occupied by railway workers and their families. In the distance on the left is the Fishery Inn.

Rough Down, from the Moor, Boxmoor

Looking across the moor, canal and London Road to Boxmoor Station, partly hidden by trees. The name was changed to Boxmoor & Hemel Hempstead in 1912, to Hemel Hempstead & Boxmoor in 1930 and Hemel Hempstead Station on 15 June 1964. The large white building is the Railway Hotel, which has been demolished and replaced by a modern glass nightclub/disco called La Mirage in 1989.

Heath Farm, *c.* 1910. Later to became Heath Barn, it is a Grade II listed building. Colonel F.S. Brereton, a writer of children's books, lived here for several years and made some alterations to the building. Previously it was a private school run Mr & Mrs Entwistle. The land and house were sold in the 1950s and it is now part of Hemel Hempstead School and used as a music centre.

St. John's Church and Harding's Bridge, *c.* 1912. Several decades later, increasing traffic from the town centre to the old A41 caused the bridge to be altered and widened. Parts of the Moor were fenced including the water's edge. This postcard was used by Tombleson's Toys, a shop in the High Street, as an advertisement to visit their shop.

Heath Park Halt, c. 1912. Shows the old Heath Park Hotel. The left-hand bridge leads to the town and the other side to Two Waters Road and the one-way street. 'Puffing Annie' seems ready to move off to Midland Station and on to Harpenden. The gentlemen's conveniences were situated below the wooden steps going up to the platform. A favourite game for local children was putting pennies on the line hoping for the train to flatten them.

Hemel Hempstead Cricket Club ground by Heath Park, 1926. The Salvation Army held their meetings here on summer evenings. Mr W.H. Charman, local butcher, is playing the side drum on the right of the photograph.

Heath Park on a misty day around the turn of the century. Boxmoor Hall was built for the community and was the venue for many public meetings. it is used regularly as an Arts Centre for young people. On the corner of Cotterells is Heath Park Hotel, once an elegant residential hotel for gentlemen and their families. It was demolished in the 1960s and a modern pub with function rooms has been built on the site. Heath Park Halt was built of wood with diagonal slatting and opened to passengers in 1905 for journeys to Redbourn and Harpenden.

Five

Schooldays

Boys of Piccott's End School with their Headmaster 'The Gaffer', 1929. The school had a garden and working in it was part of the curriculum. Joe Johnson, Frank Gomm, John Foster, Cyril Franklin, Bertram Cook, Mr Elliott (headmaster), Frank Cole, Bob Pratt, Sydney Smith, Phillip Bennett, Sydney Baker, Bill Brockett, George Scarff.

Piccotts End School Play, *c.* 1930. Those taking part part were Henry Burgess, John Budd, Miss Foxall, Mr 'Gaffer' Elliott, David Gardener, 'Wiggy' Crawley.

George Street Football and Netball Teams. Both won the cup in 1922. Headmistress Miss Kate Seabrook is in the centre.

These young ladies were never absent during the during the year of 1903 from the Hemel Hempstead Girls' National School. Franklin, Edith Seabrook, Jane Currell, -?-, Daisy Wooley. On leaving school, Jane Currell was presented with a gold watch because she was never absent or late during the whole of her school life.

George Street School Group, *c. 1922*. The school was built in 1855 and enlarged in 1876. Mabel Seabrook was Little Bo-Peep. A new school was built in 1969 to replace the old one, which later, for a time, became a Teachers' Centre.

Bury Mill End School, Astley Road. The school was built in 1877 and enlarged in 1890. In the 1960s the children were transferred to the new South Hill School and the school was for some time used for adult education. It was later demolished and a nursery school was built in its place.

Bury Mill End School, 1936. Back rows: Ted Ritman, Eric Wade, Doug Allum, Maurice Draper, Roy Dean, Horace Townsend, Cyril Coughtrey, Vic Dolling, Harry Dunham, Jack Walker, Cyril Canvin, Ray Ginger. Girls: Joan Walker, Freda Felmingham, Sybil Young, Margery Fowler, Joy Smith, Joan Attwood, Beryl Pedder, Vera Pipkin, Joan Canone, Betty Wiseman, Joyce Stranks, Olive Lockyer. Seated: Henry Godleman, Percy Pike, Linda Courtnage, Phyllis Minter, Vera Gilson, Eileen Prince, Doreen Nother, Tony Denchfield, Tom Payne. Front Row: Reg Sells, Ken Evesham, Roy Willmore, Alan Watts, Bill Jennings. Teacher: Norman Redrup.

Cowper Road infants, *c.* 1930. Edwin Bates, Freda Knight, Doreen Huckins, Kath Wheeler, Sid Leek, Frank Ball, Renee Leek, Stella Watmore, Harry Fisher, Peter Howse, Peter Batchelor, Barbara Layton, Gilbert Hitchcock, Eric Newton. Front row: Margaret Bateman, Daphne Clark, Joan Greenhill, Joyce Burke, Eileen Wilson, Dorothy Hickey, Nancy ?, Dennis King, Annie Fossey; each end: Ray Leek, Les Wright.

Boxmoor Infants celebrate the Queen's coronation, 1953. The small playground is decorated with flags and bunting; even the outside toilets are in disguise.

1962 was the year that Mr Staten's 'Little School' won the cup. Back row: Chrissie Craddock, Paula Lee, Maureen Bailey. Front row: Carol Bindoff and Louise Reed.

Boxmoor Infants pose for a photo along the canal when pinafores and sailor suits were fashionable, c. 1920. Behind, in the distance, can be seen what is now the Princes Arms on the London Road and Roughdown Common.

Heath Brow School, Heath Lane, a prep. school for boys from six years of age. It also had a kindergarten for both boys and girls from four years. The school was later transferred to Beechwood Park, Markyate, and the site developed for private housing.

The gymnasium at Heath Brow was sometimes used for local children to watch a film show, sitting on wooden forms. Usually these were educational or nature films, sometimes Laurel and Hardy.

Heath Brow School staff and pupils, 1943. Principal Mr G.W. Seth Ward, his wife and child, are in the centre of the group. Some of the pupils are Ian Stewart, Edward Bancroft, Brian Curtoise, Tony Weston, Roger Oakins, Peter Berlanny, Michael Armstrong, Roger Glennister, Paul Hanyside, Tony Lloyd, Gerald Mayo, Gordon & Dougie Masters, Phillip Mayo, John & Richard Lord, Peter Humphries, Richard Bickmore, Mark Boxer. The dining room is in the window on the extreme left. Upstairs are boarders' dorms.

Apsley Manor School, *c.* 1910, when most girls wore pinafores to school. It was built in 1857 and enlarged in 1905. It closed briefly in 1939 and re-opened again to take in evacuees during wartime. The school closed for good in 1949 and was later demolished.

Corner Hall School Football Team, 1946/7 season. Mr Barnard (Headmaster), Keith Ball, Brian Funnel, Eric Selden, Ivan Cripps, Richard Foskett, Archie Hosier, Mr Filbrick (sports and science master), Brian Allen, Kenny Final, John Reader, Jimmy Fletcher, Jimmy Scott.

Central School, 1936. Back row: Maurice Woolsey, ? Payne, Charles Kingsley, Reg Hoar, Ernest Dickinson, Ramond Lavender, D. Allen, James Edmunds, Peter Gee, Ron Smith, Russell Sykes, David Collier, Miss Badcock, Alan Smith. Second row: Doris Hopkinson, Diana Jameson, Barbara Mason, Madeline Leat, Vera Alder, Joan Cain, Vera Pipkin, Beryl Bailey. Front row: Leslie Hammersley, Joy Childs, Jean Edmonds, Grace Gent, Daphne Hemley, Joyce Lee, Joyce Strange, Maureen Pearce, Betty Blythe, Vera Woodward, Edna Channell, Don Groome.

St Mary's House, Central School, 1938. Back row: Jack Davis, -?-, Jean Stanley, Sheila Sapsford, Jean Irving, Diana Jamieson, Barbara Mason, -?-, Peter Gee. Middle row: Mr Barnard Head, ? Lumm, Derek Eames, Gerald Hanks, Peter Hanks, Gilbert Hitchcock, -?-, -?-, Miss Tyres. Middle row, girls: Joyce Lee, Joyce Ralphs, Daphne Hemley, -?-, -?-, Gladys Marshall, Jean Lee, -?-, Jean Kerry, Gladys Kilbey. Front row: -?-, -?-, Bob Dearman, Tony Denchfield, -?-, -?-, ? Janes, Victor Dowling.

The Grammar School (Boys Side) Hemel Hempstead.   129915.

Hemel Hempstead Grammar School soon after opening, *c.* 1931. It was officially opened by the Marchioness of Salisbury and cost £40,000 to build. First head was N.H. Screeton.

Hemel Hempstead Grammar School, summer 1952.

Pixies Hill Camp School, *c.* 1940. PC Lord is talking with boys from the Camp School Chaulden. Originally meant for London children to have a taste of fresh country air, it later became a refuge for children from West Ham to escape the bombs during the Second World War. The headmaster was Mr J. Moon. The school was well equipped with sports facilities, and the children were often treated to film shows courtesy of the USA Base at Bovingdon Airfield.

Six

At Work

Apsley Mills, 1933. Practice area before Apsley Station was built. Pictured are: F. Soar, G. Doult, F. Langston, J. Reeves, and driver F. Kerry.

Winner of the M & B Shield (National Championship) 1964. Apsley Mills Fire Brigade team. F. Boarder, P. Harman, D. Bailey, D. Dorrofield, R. Tompkins, R. Boarder, F. Payne, M. Ousley, K. James, A. Final, P. Rathbone.

Inspection at Apsley Mills Fire Station, 1948. Chief Officer was G. Blackstone (Herts County Chief). Sir Reginald Bonsor was Chairman of the company 1933–55.

Fire Protection Week, 1948. Fire engine on show at the main entrance to Apsley Mills. These stairs would be full of workers at lunchtime and home time after they had clocked (bundy) in and out.

Book Sewing Department in the late 1920s. Two of the operators are Liz Cook and Alice Sells.

The 'Mill Rush' in 1949, when hundreds of workers poured out of Apsley Mills for their dinner break or home time. Many buses were lined up ready and waiting as minutes were precious in one hour's break to take people to various parts of the town. There were also hoards of cyclists who filled the roads anxious to get home as soon as possible. This is the Main Time Office entrance and the white building is 'The Cottage' where directors and visitors dined. It also had a boardroom and the Nurse's first aid room.

H. Druce Butcher, Apsley, *c*. 1910. A seasonal display of meat, poultry, and game in the days when there were no food and health inspectors to worry about. The premises have seen many changes and its now an Indian takeaway.

Watercress Beds at Two Waters, *c*. 1905. Watercress was grown widely along the Gade and Bulbourne river valleys. A large proportion went on the train every day to the London markets. These beds belonged to Mr Williams and family. Part of the Bell pub is towards the left of the photo behind the bushes and along the London Road towards Boxmoor can be seen the pointed tower of Two Waters School.

Fosters Saw Mills, *c.* 1910, which was part of Boxmoor village life for many years. The family lived in the house fronting the canal. During 1914–18 they produced ammunition boxes for the navy called 'Ditty Boxes' and dealt with wet and dry wood. After a serious fire the mills were demolished in 1967 and flats called River Park have been built on this site.

Fosters Saw Mills, *c.*, 1957. 'Whizzle' Dan Newton, Jack Lee and Harry Steven. The wood had to be cut into suitable lengths prior to using.

Some of the workforce at Fosters, c. 1950. Back row: C. Bateman, K. Prosser, K. Jones, B. Shadbolt, R. Hall, K. Charge, J. Groom, T. Odell, G. Edmonds, F. Attwood, H. Stevens, J. Gower, V. Dolling, J. Lee, Second row: C. Meek, A. Norman, L. Cross, H. Johnson, J. Bates, P. Bradbury, E. Luck, F. Reynolds, E. Bateman, D. Gent, D. Brunt, J. Pearsall, J. Cross, E. Kirk, J. Lee, E. Gates. Third row: J. Ellis, C. Badcock, H. Palmer, D. Groom, ? Latchford, J. Elborn, G. Holiday, D. Waites, G. Plummer, G. Newton, ? Clark, H. Fliton, A. Hollick, L. Campbell. Fourth row: A. Franklin, B. Smith, T. Simon, B. House, P. Murphy, J. Gray, F. Brown, C. Edmunds, D. Newton, N. Cooley, A. Littlechild, J. Watts, ? Garner, C. Austin. Front row: F. Hicklin, P. Rance, -?-, -?-, -?-, -?-, -?-, G. Element, J. Harding, R. Palmer, E. Prentice, A. Blomfield, ? Jenkins.

Hemel Hempstead Engineering Co., 1957. The firm was founded by Joseph Cranstone in 1798 and had premises off the High Street behind the Rose & Crown. It passed from father to son and later by the Christopher family. The firm moved to larger premises in 1949 and increased the work force. The large, long sheds at the top of the picture are 'Buffer' depots where food was stored for large-scale emergencies. These premises at Cupid Green closed in 1982.

Wharf Road, 1908. This new bakery van was a great improvement on an ordinary horse-drawn cart for delivering the bread and cakes to customers.

St. John's, Boxmoor, 1926. Charman Butchers' horse and cart pose for a photograph outside their shop. Opposite is the Primitive Methodist Church that was a landmark in the village. It closed in 1958 and has been replaced by shops and garages.

Lawrence & Stainforth, c. 1920s. This grocers was in the lower part of Bury Road. Previously known as Baileys grocer and butcher, it had been established here from 1906. Mr Stainforth is on the left, Mr Lawrence, his partner, left and moved to a shop in London. The other person is Mr W. Charman, who began his own business in Boxmoor in 1926 as a butcher in St. John's Road., The whole business moved to the parade in the 1950s until it closed in the 1970s.

The Broadway, c. 1907. Shops along this half-timbered terrace were called the Broadway. The left shop was Kimich, a milliner and ladies' outfitters. Next door was Joseph Kimich, watchmaker and jeweller. The Broadway was also the home of the Hemel Hempstead Fire Brigade from 1906 to 1937 when they moved to new, larger premises in 1937 in Alexandra Road.

Marlowes, *c.* 1940s. This house at 56 Marlowes was one of the first telephone exchanges for the town. It was next door to Mr Dean, dentist. Mr & Mrs Glover and Miss Walker operated the manual switchboard on the first floor. The ground floor was the Apparatus Room. They were able to memorise all the telephone numbers on the Boxmoor Exchange. It moved to larger premises in Lamsey Road in 1965. An even earlier exchange was in in Cotterells around 1914.

D. Thorne, Coal Merchant. A family business since 1903 in St John's Road, Boxmoor, it moved further along into the village in 1947 when the Beechfield Road development took place.

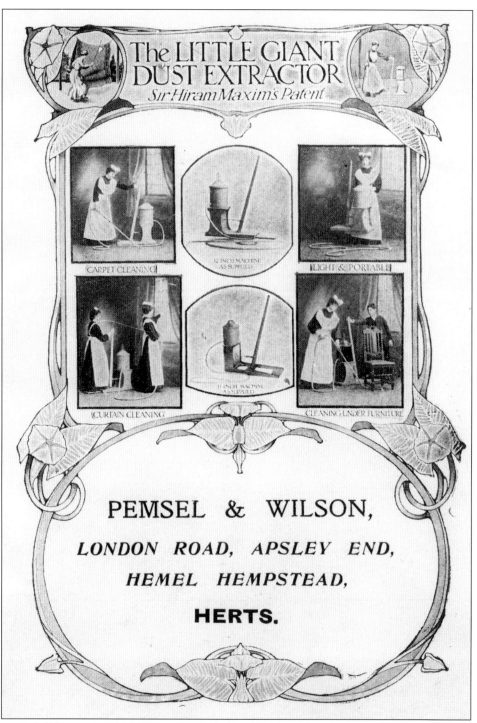

Pemsel & Wilson, c. 1905. The cover of this booklet advertises The Little Giant Dust
Extractor, which was then the latest machine before the vacuum cleaner came on the scene.
Pemsel & Wilson were the agents for this company as well as being garage owners and the first
to run a motor bus service to and from Boxmoor Station to the town.

Seven
People and Places

Gadebridge Farmhouse, c. 1900. The residence of George Reay, steward to Sir Astley Paston-Cooper. Mrs George Reay is standing by the gate.

George Reay (born 1847) in his councillor's robes. He lived at Gadebridge Home Farm from 1900 to 1912. In 1906 he was steward to Lt Col. Lionel Paston-Cooper and was later a farmer in his own right. The original photo was taken by P.T. Culverhouse, whose studios were in the High Street, Hemel Hempstead.

Gadebridge House, which was built about the turn of the seventeenth century, once belonged to the Combes as a farmhouse. It had been enlarged and altered over the years. Sir Astley Paston-Cooper owned and occupied the house in the early nineteenth century. He founded the Infirmary at Piccotts End in 1826. Another Sir Astley was the first Mayor of the Borough in 1896. The grounds were bought from the estate by the Council in 1952.

A mothers' Union outing to Gadebridge House, c. 1901. Lady Drake is in the centre of the photograph holding a basket. Feel sorry for the babies, wearing all those clothes!

Lord and Lady Drake and their sons in the grounds of Gadebridge House, 1895.

Staff of Northridge, home of Nathaniel Micklem QC, JP, *c.* 1911. Including Mr Tripp, Mr & Mrs Moore, Reg Moore, Ethel, Violet, Dorothy, and Florence Timberlake, Miss Sibley, Mr and Mrs Herbert, Reg Clark and his mother, Herbert Wren, Mrs Higgins, Ada Joliffe, Sis Sirrett.

Rally at Northridge, Boxmoor, *c.* 1910. Mr Micklem was the Liberal candidate for West Herts. He opposed the New Town Plan of 1946. An enquiry was held in 1949 when he was almost one hundred years old; in spite of his age he put his objections over clearly, and with energy.

Corner Hall, once owned by Edwardian author and playwright William John Locke. His wife was an actress. The drive began where Cedar Walk is now.

Three Gables, Corner Hall, *c.* 1908, home of the Sanguinetti family since 1906. The young girl sitting in the garden is believed to be Nancy Sanguinetti aged eight. The previous owners were the Deacon family who lived there until 1858 when the Woodman family came. The building is a fifteenth-century house and was a resting place for pilgrims. It had been threatened with demolition, but is now offices.

Three inmates of St Pauls (known by locals as The Base). The man in the centre is Tommy Cook who was a rag and bone man, he used his donkey as a lawnmower! The Union Workhouse has seen many changes since it was first built in 1836 when there was space for one hundred paupers. It was used as an emergency hospital during the Second World War. It is now demolished to make way for houses.

St. Paul's Elderly/Sick Ward, Christmas 1938. The wards were used by Great Ormond Street and eventually became the Maternity Unit. Matron Mrs Grayer, on the right, and Sister Turner, on the left, who married Mr Curwen, the Assistant Relief Officer for Poor Law Institution.

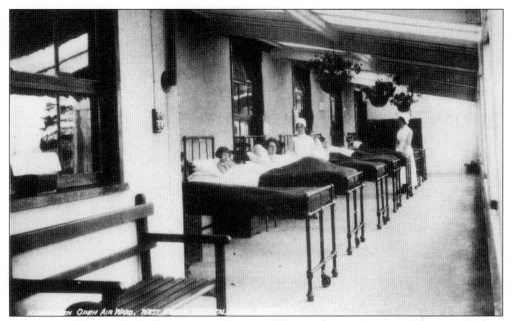

A successful Harpenden Village Fair resulted in £500 being raised for West Herts Hospital. A ward of 30 beds, mainly for TB patients, was opened on 20 September 1924. It was named Harpenden Open Air Ward and had large expanses of glass windows that could be opened very wide.

Curie Ward, St. Paul's, 1965. Sister Minty, Bill Minty (Deputy Administrator), Keith Minty, Staff Nurse Hogan, and other staff all help to give out the Christmas dinner to the patients.

Young lads of the town only too happy to dress up for a good cause and collect money for the Hospital Fund which relied heavily on donations and collections on Bank Holidays.

Members of the Red Cross, ready with their collecting tins, standing outside the ladies' changing room at Churchill Swimming Pool, c. 1950s.

The Swimming Pool, Hemel Hempstead

129977.

Churchill Swimming Pool was opened on 1 May 1937 on a cold and misty morning. The water was not heated in the early days, but that did not prevent youngsters competing to be first in on the morning the season began each year. Mr Whittle, the superintendent, was always on hand to see everyone behaved. The large buildings were the changing rooms, filled with lockers for clothes.

Heath Park, 21 February 1920. There was an official ceremony of handing over a First World War tank to the Borough in recognition of record war savings. It was set by the junction of St John's Road and Station Road where the War Memorial now stands. Scoutmaster E.H. Lidderdale can be seen in his uniform front right of the photograph.

Brunswick Place, Boxmoor, *c.* 1910. A small alley leading to four cottages tucked behind the Steamcoach pub. These ladies are outworkers for G.B. Kent & Sons of Apsley, hand-making brushes outside their front door.

The Anchor Pub in Anchor Lane, when it was just a lane. This view was taken before Beechfield Road and Anchor Lane had houses built in this part of Boxmoor, around 1947. At one time the pub had a very large piece of Hertfordshire Pudding Stone near the front door.

Some of the regulars outside the Old Anchor Pub in Anchor Lane. The man with the dog was Ern Cox the dog's name was Wops. They were always together. The young man with the bicycle was Ern's son, Ernie Cox, who later became a local builder. The landlord at this time – between 1910 and 1920 – was William Todd. It was demolished in the early 1950s, when Beechfield Road was built and Anchor Lane was widened. A new pub was built with the same name on the corner of these two roads.

Crabtree School, 1942. Members of the Air Training Corp 1178 SQ. Meetings were held at the school. Names include Roy Burnell, Bill Norman, Ken Parrott, Cecil Sykes, Colin Crawley, Gordon Freeman, Billy Gower, Ken Lovell, Maurice Pocock, Maurice Woolsey, Ronald Thurnam, David Collier, Peter Stacey, Russell Sykes, Den King, Ben Carpenter, ? Giddings, Alfred Harris, Jimmy Dove. The masters are Mr Lawrence and Mr Barnard.

Eight

Churches

Revd F.O. Houseman and Revd L.G. Tucker (curate) of St. Mary's Church, Apsley, with a few of their parishioners, *c.* 1912.

Box Lane Chapel has had worshippers here in Box Lane for over 350 years. The Oak Gates were erected in memory of Ernest Phillips, who was killed in a motor bike accident. His father was life-deacon at the church. This photo was found among papers of Mr Francis Moore, who was treasurer of the Chapel in 1913. The building closed its doors in June 1969 and has been converted into a private house.

Members of Miss Clapton's Bible Class at St John's, c. 1950s. Back row: Shirley Draper, Joan Dimmock, Barbara Hammond, Olive Mason, Judith Butcher, Janet Priestnall, Pamela Palfrey, Barbara Dean, Denise Grass. Middle row: Linda Draper, Joan Waters, Sheila Gray, Muriel Holiday, Pamela Weaver, Marion Waite, -?-, Christine Ogden, Valerie Cheshire, Wendy Hosier, Celia Nightingale, -?-, Christine Waters, Ann Westfield. Front row: Brenda Lee, Ann Mason, Josephine Roberts, Christine Meakins, Miss M. Clapton, -?-, Gwen Weaver, Joyce Groom, Janet Weaver.

St John's Church, Boxmoor, *c.* 1900. This replaced an earlier Chapel-of-Ease dated 1829. The present church was dedicated in 1874 and enlarged in 1893. The first vicar was Revd A.C. Richings, until 1899. The wall and railings have long since gone and been replaced by landscaped gardens of flower beds and shrubs.

St John's Church choir, 1948. Some of the members are Louis Rew, ? Crawley, ? Hosier, John Pointer, Charles Mailing, ? Collier, William Waite, James Elborn, Gerald Groom, Ernie Hannant, George Cheshire (Choirmaster) Canon C.C. Hamilton (Vicar), Harry Cooper, Henry Charge, Donald Baker, Ted Cox, Charles Mailing Jnr, Colin Wackett, ? Picton. Canon Hamilton was vicar from 1927 to 1962.

The new Church of St. Francis, opened in July 1914. Some of the surrounding large trees have been felled and in 1948 Beechfield Road and housing estate linked up with this part of Hammerfield, making it more accessible.

Members of St. Francis's Church and choir, c. 1943. Mr Povey, Michael Harding, L. Scarfe, Mr Gulliver, Mr Lindley, Father Hindley, Mr Brett, Mr Pratt, Mr Millington, Graham Whitlock, Mr Stewart, Mr Cooper, Michael Latchford, Keith Barton, John Lindley, Ian Stewart, Andrew Scarfe, Peter Harding, Gerald Rolph, Peter Garner, Stewart Scarfe.

olic Church, Boxmoor.

The Catholic Church of St. Mary & St. Joseph, late 1940s. This church in Boxmoor was first opened in 1898, although Mass had been held earlier in 1893 in a cottage in the village. Alterations and extensions have been made and with the road-widening scheme the main entrance was moved to the side of the building.

The Methodist Church, 1958. This Church was first opened on 11 November 1869 and became an important part of village life. In 1939 the chapel became a reception area for evacuees, also a place of worship for soldiers and German POWs on parole from a local camp. It was closed in 1958 when the new and larger Bourne Methodist Church was opened in Chaulden Northridge Way.

The vicar of St. Mary's Parish Church was Revd Lawrence Gee. This is a photograph of his wife and children, 1898. He remained as vicar there until 1920.

The parish church of St. Mary's dates back to 1150 when it was dedicated. It is one of the finest examples of Norman architecture in the country. The fluted leaden spire erected in the early fourteenth century has been recently restored.

Civic Service at St. Mary's, *c.* 1945. Mayor Alfred Lewis Selden, Town Clerk, C.W.G.T. Kirk and Alderman A.H. Jarman were all well-known local dignitaries of the town.

99

The Congregational Church, Alexandra Road. This was built in 1890, replacing an iron chapel supplied by Mr Cranstone of the High Street foundry in 1880. The land was previously owned by the Paston-Cooper family for development in this part of Hemel Hempstead called the 'New Town'.

Nine

Freetime

Apsley Football Club winners 1923/4 season for the Apsley Charity Cup and Watford Hospital Shield. They played on Salmon Meadow.

Apsley FC 1904/5. Winners of West Herts League Divisions One and Two and St. Mary's Cup. Back row, left to right: William Beck, M.T. Mackay, S. Gurney, C.H. Hawkins, E. Gurney, A.E. Hazell, F. Tyers. Second row: A. Allum, S. Findlay, D. Bandle, G. Coxhill, A. Janes, W.R. Beck, G. Picton, G. Dowse, F. King, S. Parnell, D. Birchmore. Third row: G.F. Seagrave (Assistant Honorary Secretary), J. Homans, W. Butler, H. Kempster, F. Jackson, J. Sparrow, W. Coker J. Paton, W. Tyers (Honorary Secretary). Front row: A. Hay, A. Gurney, -?-, H. Chennells, C. Green, A. Kitchener, G. Theed, S.W. Tuckwell.

The White Lion darts team, 1947. Bob Beecroft is the man in the dark hat. The pub was in Queensway. The site has been redeveloped for offices.

Boxmoor Hockey XI March 1949. Taken at Hemel Hempstead Grammar School, the team did not have a home ground and had to play all away fixtures. This led to the eventual break-up about a year after this photograph was taken.

Hemel Hempstead Bowls Club, 1938. Back row: W.H. Horne, W. Price-Jones, -?-, Bernard Keen, -?-. Middle row: S. Higgins, T.F. Poulter, Bill Brockett, W. Stainforth, -?- Wilf E. Davies, -?-, Sid Monk, A. Harry Jarman, -?-, Seated: -?-, Revd C.C. Dawson, A.E. Hazell, Billy Crook, Warren Osborne, W. Fells, H.E. Webbs, A.C. Cripps (Secretary).

Hemel Hempstead Bowls Club Winners, 1953. Standing, H.H. Hall (Secretary), S.C. Monk (Skip), W., Walley, Bill Brockett,, Frank Caslake. Seated: Ernie Smith, Freddy Butterfield, Reg Saunders (Captain), Warren Osborne. This photograph was taken in front of the new pavilion at 2 Queensway.

Hemel Hempstead Bowls Club showing Pavilion and grounds situated behind the shops in the Parade, Marlowes, 1957.

The Ladies' Section of Hemel Hempstead Bowls Club, 1967, which was formed in 1946. Members include Sheillah Tatton, Mrs Wiseman, Gladys Savage, Mary Poulter, Ada Petherick, Dot Francis, Elsie Fair, Nora Copeman, Lily Glover, Molly Begbie, Joan Stone Front row: Ethel Smith (Captain), Marion Parslow, Joyce Whittle (Treasurer), Mary England (Secretary) handing bouquet to Margaret Walker (President).

Boxmoor School Cup Winners, 1925. Back row: Ag Newton, Dan Crawley, George Bateman, Den Gower, Tom Final, Bill Barber. Front: Den Clarke, George Smith, Stan Sherfield, Phil Preston, Cecil Ambrose, George Harmsworth. The identity of the boy in 'civvies' is a mystery.

Boys Sports Team Corner Hall School, Crabtree Lane, *c.* 1945. Mr Barnard (Headmaster), Bob Scarborough, Alfie Howard, Peter Hemley, Roy Walker, and Alan Dell are some of the boys. Mr Philbrick is the sports and science master.

Boxmoor St John's Football Team proudly showing off their trophies outside the 'Steamer' pub in St John's Road, c. 1930.

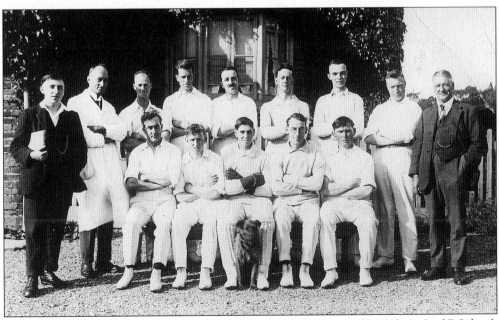

Boxmoor Cricket Club, c. 1930. Outside the Headmaster's House of St. John's C of E School. St. John's Hall was built next door in 1932.

Bovingdon Boys' Harmonica Band, early 1930s. Local lads were brought together by the respected village policeman PC Donald Lord. Members included Donald Beeson, Burt Bevan, Bob Burgin, John Gurney, Phil Gurney, Stan Harris, Peter Hill, Harold Housecoe, Basil Lake, Peter Puddiphat, Charles Rance Cyril Roberts, Jim Teasdale, Dickie Watson.

Photograph taken by P.T. Culverhouse, High Street. The accordian band included Harold Sells, Fred Whittaker, Bill Minty, Bill Hollick, Ken Ball, Alan Watts, Reg Walker, John ?, Ken Glover. c. 1935.

House of Dickinson Band, 1932–3. Taken in the grounds near the cottage. Some of the bandsmen are Ted Cleveland, Wes Gurney, Bill Harrington, Tom House, Bob Seabrook, Charles Selden, George Gurney, Sydney Phipps, George Stubbington, George Plummer, Alfred Goodman (Bandmaster), Percy Stevens, Fred Gurney, Jack Owen, Stan Amos, Frank Reeves, Bill Pearman, Jack Newland, M. Streete, Ivor Clayton, George Ringshall, Les Ayres (drummer), Eric Watts, Cliff Thorne, Frank Leahy, Frank Clark, Bob Croup.

At the Boy Scout Rally, 1914. E.H. Lidderdale, County Commissioner, West Herts. District. Two of the dignitaries who attended were Lord Clarendon and Sir Ernest Shackleton.

Off to camp, 1921. Some of the scouts with 'Nunc' to summer camp.

Third Boxmoor Scout Troop outside Headquarters, Woodland Avenue. Mr Bell was the Scoutmaster, summer 1956.

VJ Day, 15 August 1945. The Boxmoor Guides were based at The Poplars, Cowper Road, then a Roman Catholic Nunnery. Mother Anne Winifrede, Elizabeth Trye, Sheila Klesel, Jean Ellis, Christine and Gillian Reynolds, Anita ?, Theresa Streeton, Rosemary Trye, Margaret Walshe, Mary Presland, Pamela Truett, Margaret Newton, Anne Gates, Valerie Cheshire.

St John's Bible Class Cricket Team between 1917 and 1927, when Revd Smith-Cranmoor was vicar. Harry Holloway, Mr Jenkins, Colin Abrahams, Ernest Lupton, Jack Poulter, ? Dyer, 'Wiggy' How, Percy Hoar and dog, Les Jordan. The vicarage in Heath Lane is in the background.

Ten
Special Days

Hand-folding section of the Envelope Dept., Apsley, on an outing to Edlesborough, 18 September 1915.

Boxmoor hall, 24 February 1912. A dinner given to the employees of the British Paper
Company in celebration of their 21st year of formation at Frogmore Mill. Managing Director
Mr C.H. Sanguinetti, Miss Woodman, Mrs Pitts, Mr F.A. Rudall (Director), Mrs Bateman, Mr
H.P. Bateman, Mrs Sanguinetti and Mr E. Pitts (Manager) were other members of the company
on the top table.

One of the elaborate Coronation Arches at Frogmore Apsley, 1911.

This entry for a decorated cycle won a well-deserved first prize at the Apsley & Nash Mills Coronation celebrations, 1911. Amazingly, the cycle could be ridden.

A procession along London Road, Apsley, postmarked 1905. St. Mary's Church can just be seen in the distance. The building on the extreme right is the Oddfellows Arms.

Heath Park hotel is decorated for a special event, *c.* 1900. It was an elegant building that catered for gentlemen and their families. Boxmoor Hall was built in the Flemish style in 1890. This gathering is at the junction of St John's Road and Station Road, Boxmoor.

Hospitals were always needing charitable efforts for raising funds. Subscriptions and gifts in kind were always welcomed. Even the bad weather could not prevent this Hospital Demonstration taking place. This postcard, dated 28 August 1910, was printed and posted less than a week later on 2 September.

One of the many floats waiting to move off to take part in fund raising for the local hospital. The windows of Boxmoor Hall are recognisable in the background. These processions usually assembled and began from St. John's Road.

Boxmoor Pageant, 26 and 27 July 1922, which was held at Lockers Park to help raise money for Boxmoor St John's New Hall. Many well-known members of the community took part including the Brockman family, Frank S. Badcock and E.H. Lidderdale.

Third Boxmoor Scout Troop were also involved in the Boxmoor Pageant of 1922. Patrol leader Jock was Master Francis Combe. The story of the Pageant covered many years of Hemel Hempstead's past history.

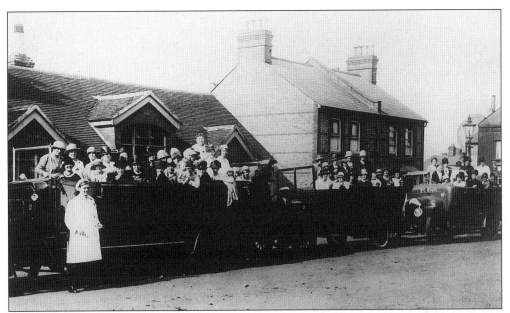

Mothers' Union outing ready to move off from outside the Church Parish Rooms in Horsecroft Road. The Rooms were the scene of many bible class meetings and sales of work. It was also a soup kitchen in times of need, where a bowl of soup could be had for ½d. When St. John's Hall was built in 1932, the rooms became a working men's club. Today, it is Boxmoor Social Club.

Bream coaches ready to take ladies from the White Lion Pub on an outing, c. 1940. Charlie Knight was the owner of the business, he owned a fish and chip shop in Marlowes, therefore Bream was a suitable name for the company. Charlie Eveson was usually the driver. Some of the ladies are Mrs Groome, Mrs Cooper, Mrs Lamb, Mrs Hosier, Miss Pat Cross, Mrs Claridge, Mrs Ginger with Clive, Mrs Bricknell.

Prince of Wales visit July 1926. The Prince came to Hemel Hempstead to attend a centenary reception at the Town Hall before going on to the West Herts Hospital. He was welcomed by the Mayor, Henry Anderson.

Prince of Wales visits West Herts Hospital to lay a foundation stone at the new Maternity Building, July 1926. Miss Semphill was the matron. he also found time in his busy schedule to see other wards and people. The patients pictured here are wearing war medals.

An important day for Hemel Hempstead New Town, when H.M. Queen Elizabeth II visited the town. She visited a family in one of the new houses. She was accompanied by the Bishop of St. Albans for the Foundation Stone ceremony.

Members of the Red Cross lined up in Adeyfield Square for HM the Queen, who came to Hemel Hempstead on July 20 1952 to lay a foundation stone of St. Barnabas. The square was later renamed Queen's Square after her visit.

Members of John Dickinson (Apsley) Band, 1951, winners of the *Daily Herald* Brass Band Championship at Belle Vue. Bill Gurney (Bandmaster), D. Hoar, Jim Page, David Sennitt, F. Gibbs, D. Wigham, Cliff Thorne, Wes Gurney, Bill Gomm, Peter Davis, Sonny Briggs, B. Goodman, Tony Britton, Ray Grimsdale, Roy Hollick, Phil Catlinet (Conductor), H. Goodman, Bob Seabrook, John Copcutt, Fred Kibble, Brian Hollick, Ted Cleveland and son Ivor, Dougie Wilson, W. Briggs and D. Cripps.

Boxmoor Silver Band passing the War Memorial at The Plough, *c.* 1950. Bert Rolph, Basil Wicks, Ernest Jordan, John Mew, Bert Mayo, Bill Waite, Harold Hunt, Alf Cook, Reg Sear, Eric Elborn, George Gilbert, George Hunt, Bill Mills, Sid Green, Tom Mills.

Members of the Hemel Hempstead Amateur Operatic and Dramatic Society, *c.* 1949. Ready to join the annual procession through the town to Gadebridge Park. Pamela East, Len Hopkins, Lorna Mojon, Molly Harries, Fred Lane. This year – 1995 – is the seventieth anniversary of their formation in 1925.

Tables and chairs set out in Puller Road, Boxmoor, for the street party in 1945.

VE Day, August 1945. Children and neighbours of Puller Road pose for this special street party to mark the end of the war in Europe. In spite of rations and shortages, plenty of food was found for this event.

A group of neighbours, friends, and children in Puller Road, Boxmoor, celebrate the Coronation of Queen Elizabeth II in 1953. The old brick building was thought to have been a store for straw used for straw plait, later it was used as garages. Mrs Floyd, Mrs Element Mrs Whitfield, Hettie Lee, Mrs Shaw, Kenny Dawdy, Tony Dunn, Jackie Gurney, Mrs Bateman, Brenda and Eileen Bates, Mr Weight, Mrs F. Newton, Mrs Maize, Mrs Leech, Mrs Daisy Newton, Mrs Sear and Ian, Mrs Stone, Glenda and Mary Harrington, Rodney Gillan, Stella Lee, Ann Lye, Peter Harrington, Ann Dawdy, Pauline Dunn, Barry Dunn, Mrs Hicks, Rose Walton, Minnie Gillan, Mrs Bass, Win Lee. Children: Christine Jones, Ronnie Littlechild, Queen Ann Butterfield, Pat Lee with Peter and Theresa.

May Day, *c.* 1925. Children from Boxmoor School celebrate May Day on the Moor wearing their best clothes and carrying baskets and posies of flowers. The highlight of the day was the crowning of the May Queen.

H.G. Charlton was first prize winner for best turn out; he had a small place behind the premises in the High Street. The dairy was later taken over by Fred Radford. In those days, *c.* 1930, there were often two deliveries a day, one very early and the second round came mid-morning, called 'The Pudding Round'.

'The Patch' in Puller Road with members of the Dart Team and their trophies, 1957. H. Floyd, Ron Charge, Fred Prestland, Bert Stannard, Peter Duncan, Maurice Newton, Perc. Fuller, Den Palmer, Vic Floyd (with cup), Keith Sexton, Taff Craddock, Reg Gold, Nobby Goodwin, Stan Smith, Harry Clark, Fred Redman, Jack Priestley, Jack Lee, Bill Lee.

Ladies' outing from 'The Patch' (Post Office Arms) in Puller Road, *c.* 1957. Mrs Charge, Mrs Reed, Mrs Bradman, Mrs Searle, Mrs Sexton, Mrs Newton, Pat Fuller, Mrs Impey, Mrs Floyd, Mrs Cross, Mrs Ambrose, Mrs Stannard, Mrs Redman, Mrs Goodwin, Mrs Holliman, Cynthia Lee, Mrs Lee.